NATIONAL GEOGRAPHIC

Heat Changes Things

Harley Chan

What melts ice cream?

Heat melts ice cream.

What cooks the eggs?

Heat cooks the eggs.

What makes the clothes smooth?

Heat makes the clothes smooth.

Heat dries my hair.

What keeps me warm?

Heat keeps me warm.

Heat changes things.